D0940997

From: Uncle Orange
& Auntie Dana

Jan, 1st 2012

WISDOM FROM
It's Not Easy Being Green

And Other Things to Consider

JIM HENSON,
THE MUPPETS, AND FRIENDS

•INTRODUCTION BY CHERYL HENSON•

PETER PAUPER PRESS, INC.
WHITE PLAINS, NEW YORK

The text in this book is excerpted from
It's Not Easy Being Green: And Other Things to Consider
by Jim Henson, The Muppets, and Friends,
originally published by Hyperion in 2005.

Designed by La Shae V. Ortiz

Published in 2007 by arrangement with Hyperion.
Peter Pauper Press, Inc.
202 Mamaroneck Avenue
White Plains, NY 10601
ISBN 978-1-59359-875-4
Printed in China
7 6 5 4 3 2 1

Visit us at www.peterpauper.com

WISDOM FROM

It's Not Easy Being Green

And Other Things to Consider

Contents

Introduction
by Cheryl Henson

The song that my dad is best known for performing is "It's Not Easy Bein' Green," written by his long-term collaborator, Joe Raposo. We chose to use it as the title of this book because its lyrics capture not only the feelings of Kermit the Frog, but a universal message that resonates with people the world over, a message that it's okay to be different, to embrace what makes you special, and to be proud of it.

What you will find in these pages is a collection of quotes, many of them from my dad's characters and creative partners. We felt that this was the best approach because the world knew my father through the Muppet characters that he performed and the words of the writers with whom he worked. But this book also contains a lot of quotes from Jim himself that have been taken from interviews, personal notebooks, letters, and other writings, some being published now for the first time.

My dad's life was full of blessings. The

unique way he approached life made it possible for him to create some of the most beloved characters the world has known and to use them to spread social values that were important to him, such as inclusiveness, tolerance, humor, and kindness. This book is intended to convey the many facets of my dad's being and his thinking. I hope you enjoy it.

— *Cheryl Henson*

Listen to
Your Heart

I believe that we form our own lives, that we create our own reality, and that everything works out for the best. I know I drive some people crazy with what seems to be ridiculous optimism, but it has always worked out for me.

– *Jim*

It's not that easy bein' green
Having to spend each day the
    color of the leaves,
When I think it might be nicer
    being red, or yellow, or gold
Or something much more colorful
    like that

It's not easy bein' green
It seems you blend in with so
    many other ordinary things
And people tend to pass you over,
'cause you're not standing out like
    flashy sparkles on the water,
    or stars in the sky

But green is the color of spring
And green can be cool and
    friendly like
And green can be big like an
    ocean
Or important like a mountain
Or tall like a tree

When green is all there is to be,
It could make you wonder why.
But why wonder, why wonder?
I am green, and it'll do fine
And I think it's what I want to be

— Kermit

The words say "It's not easy being green," but the song is about knowing who you are. And in it you hear Jim's message most clearly. He believed that people are good and that they want to do their best and that no matter how or why we might be different from anybody else, we should learn to love who we are and be proud of it.

– *Ray Charles*

A LIST OF GOOD THINGS ABOUT BEING A FROG

- Being Green
- Sitting in the sun on a lily pad
- Having thousands of brothers and sisters
- Going to the hop
- Playing leapfrog
- Having bears and pigs and dogs and chickens as your friends
- Getting kissed by princesses hoping to turn you into a handsome prince

– Kermit

We *see* with our eyes.
We *know* with our hearts.
Outside . . . Inside.

– *Cantus Fraggle*

I spend a few minutes in meditation and prayer each morning. I find that this really helps me to start the day with a good frame of reference. As part of my prayers, I thank whoever is helping me — I'm sure somebody or something is — I express gratitude for all my blessings and I try to forgive the people that I'm feeling negative toward. I try hard not to judge anyone, and I try to bless everyone who is a part of my life, particularly anyone with whom I am having any problems.

– *Jim*

But, you've heard enough.
Now, it's time for you to
listen. Go and find
your songs.

— *Cantus Fraggle*

I think there are lots of ways of leading very good lives and growing spiritually. This process of growth goes on whether we believe in it or not.

– *Jim*

Dynamite Determination

KA-BLAM!

There are no rules, and
those are the rules.

— *Cantus Fraggle*

I cannot say why I am good at what I do, but I can say that I work very hard at it. Nor am I aware of any conscious career decisions. I've always found that one thing leads to another, and that I've moved from project to project in a natural progression.

Perhaps one thing that has helped me in achieving my goals is that I sincerely believe in what I do, and get great pleasure from it. I feel very fortunate because I can do what I love to do.

— Jim

I don't resent working long hours. I shouldn't—I'm the one who set up my life this way. I love to work. It's the thing that I get the most satisfaction out of—and probably what I do best. Not that I don't enjoy days off. I love vacations and loafing around. But I think much of the world has the wrong idea of working. It's one of the good things in life. The feeling of accomplishment is more real and satisfying than finishing a good meal—or looking at one's accumulated wealth.

– Jim

I guess I was wrong
when I said
I never promised anyone.
I promised me.

— *Kermit*

Look at all those people out there. Lots of people. But my friends . . . my friends are all gone. Well, I'm, I'm going to get 'em back. I'm gonna get 'em back! 'Cause the show's not dead as long as I believe in it. And I'm gonna sell that show. And we're all gonna be on Broadway! You hear me, New York? We're gonna be on Broadway! Because, because I'm not giving up! I'm still here and

I'm stayin'! You hear that, New York? I'm stayin' here. The frog is stayin'.

— *Kermit*

This frog has a song

to be sung.
This frog isn't gonna spend his life
in a swamp
Catchin' flies with his tongue.
This frog may slip and stumble,
But this frog tries again.
This frog will never grumble,
But fall to rise again.
This frog is staying with it
Like a tick sticks to a dog.
I'm gonna win!
You're gonna love this frog!

— *Kermit*

When I was a tadpole
there was really only one
thing that I collected.
I had a file of
newspaper and magazine
articles on Frogs in Show
Business. It was a small
collection, but I think it
influenced me a lot.

– *Kermit*

Well, when the path

is steep and stony and the
night is all around
And the way that you must take is
far away
When your heart is lost and lonely
and the map cannot be found
Here's a simple little spell that you
can say:

You've got to face facts, act fast
on your own

Preparation, perspiration,
    dynamite determination
Pack snacks, make tracks all alone
Don't be cute. Time to scoot.
    Head out to your destination.

Chase the future, face the great
    unknown.

– *Gobo Fraggle*

Together
We'll Nab It

Yeah, well, I've got a dream too. But it's about singing and dancing and making people happy. That's the kind of dream that gets better the more people you share it with. And, well, I've found a whole bunch of friends who have the same dream. And it kind of makes us like a family.

— *Kermit*

Certainly we look for creativity and a sense of humor, people who have a positive view of the world, that kind of thing. We look for people that work collaboratively. It's not just me doing this stuff, it's a lot of us creating it, writers and designers and puppeteers. We have a good time working together too.

– *Jim*

Kermit's function
on this show is very
much like my own in
that he's trying to hold
together this group of
crazies. And that's not
unlike what I do.

— *Jim*

Wake up in the morning
Get yourself to work.
Fraggles never fool around.
Fraggles never shirk.
Your duty's always waiting
And duty must be done.
There's Ping-Pong games that
        must be played
And songs that must be sung.

– Gobo and the Fraggles

A film is not done by one person. It's done by a lot of people. I love this whole collaborative aspect. When it works well, you end up with something better than any of us started out to do.

– Jim

Dance your cares
away, worry's for
another day.
Let the Music play down at
Fraggle Rock.
Work your cares away,
dancing's for another day.
Work your cares away down
at Fraggle Rock.

— *The Fraggles*

There is a sense of our characters caring for each other and having respect for each other. A positive feeling. A positive view of life. That's a key to everything we do. I believe that everything we do should have part of that. Sometimes we're too heavy in terms of ourselves and trying to carry an idea, and telling kids what life is about. I often have to tell myself that too.

— *Jim*

Whenever characters become self-important or sentimental in the Muppets, then there's always another character there to blow them up immediately.

– *Frank Oz*

Moving right along

In search of good times
And good news,
With good friends you can't lose.
This could become a habit.

Opportunity just knocked,
Let's reach out and grab it,
Together we'll nab it,
We'll hitch-hike, bus, or yellow
    cab it.

— *Kermit and Fozzie*

It Starts When We're Kids

It starts when we're kids,
  a show-off in school;
Makin' faces at friends,
  you're a clown and a fool.
Doin' pratfalls and birdcalls
  and bad imitations;
Ignoring your homework,
  now that's dedication.
You work to the mirror, you're
  getting standing ovations.
You're burning with hope,
  you're building up steam.

What was once juvenilish is
  grown-up and stylish,
You're close to your dream.
Then somebody out there
  loves you,
Stands up and hollers
  for more;
You found a home at the
  Magic Store.

— *The Muppets*

When I was young, my ambition was to be one of the people who made a difference in this world. My hope still is to leave the world a little bit better for my having been here.

It's a wonderful life and I love it.

– *Jim*

As children, we all live in a world of imagination, of fantasy, and for some of us that world of make-believe continues into adulthood. Certainly I've lived my whole life through my imagination. But the world of imagination is there for all of us — a sense of play, of pretending, of wonder. It's there with us as we live.

– *Jim*

I believe that we can use television and film to be an influence for good; that we can help to shape the thoughts of children and adults in a positive way. As it turned out, I am very proud of some of the work we've done, and I think we can do many more good things.

— Jim

Be proud of your flippers
And the flies that you catch
And the logs that you leap
And the eggs you will hatch.
We're under the stars
And we're smaller than men
But I'm proud to be one of the
frogs in the glen.

– *Kermit*

The most sophisticated
people I know—inside
they're all children.
We never really lose
a certain sense we had
when we were kids.

– Jim

I've found that children keep their imaginations a lot longer than parents think they do. Parents are concerned that if kids see that a person operates the Muppet, an illusion will be shattered. But I think kids see us as just the people who carry their friends around.

— *Kevin Clash*

That attitude you have as a parent is what your kids will learn from more than what you tell them. They don't remember what you try to teach them.

They remember what you are.

– *Jim*

Here's some simple advice: Always be yourself. Never take yourself too seriously. And beware of advice from experts, pigs, and members of Parliament.

– *Kermit*

I really do believe that all of you are at the beginning of a wonderful journey. As you start traveling down that road of life, remember this: There are never enough comfort stops. The places you're going to are never on the map. And once you get that map out, you won't be able to refold it no matter how smart you are.

So forget the map, roll down the windows, and whenever you can, pull over and have a picnic with a pig. And if you can help it, never fly as cargo.

— *Kermit*

I believe that life is basically a process of growth—that we go through many lives, choosing those situations and problems that we will learn through.

– *Jim*

No time is wasted time.

– **Cantus Fraggle**

A Part of Everything and Everyone

I find that it's very important for me to stop every now and then and get recharged and reinspired. The beauty of nature has been one of the great inspirations in my life. Growing up as an artist, I've always been in awe of the incredible beauty of every last bit of design in nature. The wonderful color schemes of nature that always work harmoniously are particularly dazzling to me. I love to lie in an open field looking up at the sky. One of my happiest moments of inspiration came to me many years ago as I lay on the grass, looking up into the leaves and branches of a big old tree in California. I remember feeling very much a part of everything and everyone.

— *Jim*

When the week is

finally over,
It is wonderful to go
And putter in my garden
Where I watch the flowers grow.

It is pleasant in my garden
As I cultivate my seeds;
I plant and hoe and water
And I clear away the weeds.

Though it's frantic at the theater,
Here I leave that all behind,

And the calm within my garden
Gives this frog some peace
of mind.

– Kermit

If our "message" is anything, it's a positive approach to life. That life is basically good. People are basically good.

– Jim

I have a lot of great memories from the swamp. I remember when I was little, we'd all just sit out on our lily pads for hours and hours, rocking gently on the water and listening to the soft, sweet sound of chirping crickets . . . Then, of course, we'd eat the crickets . . . but that's another story.

— *Kermit*

I believe in taking a positive attitude toward the world, toward people, and toward my work. I think I'm here for a purpose. I think it's likely that we all are, but I'm only sure about myself. I try to tune myself in to whatever it is that I'm supposed to be, and I try to think of myself as a part of all of us—all mankind and all life. I find it's not easy to keep these lofty thoughts in mind as the day goes by, but it certainly helps me a great deal to start out this way.

— *Jim*

Show me the light
in a butterfly's eye
And show me the dreams of
the earth and the sky

Show me the night, show me the
day
Show me the secret that dances
away
There's a rainbow I wish I could
climb like a tree
A bug and a boulder that beckon
to me

Show me leaves in the spring
Show me love on the wing
Show me things that I long to
    explore
Show me more.

— *Mokey Fraggle*

He didn't have much time for quiet contemplation, but he took it wherever he could. He could stretch out a moment, looking out at the nice weather from his window above Central Park, and you knew he was really aware. Sometimes he expressed the desire for a simpler life, like when he admired the job of the man who walks along the road picking up trash with a long stick. He thought that guy had a great job, walking along with a stick (my father loved walking sticks), enjoying the road, and doing only good in the world, with hundreds of small actions.

— Lisa Henson

Yes, it's one of
the basic truths of the
physical universe,
Sprocket. Things don't
disappear. They just
change, and change,
and change again.

— *Doc, from* **Fraggle Rock**

Life's like a movie, write your
    own ending
Keep believing, keep pretending
We've done just what we set
    out to do
Thanks to the lovers, the dreamers,
    and you.

– *Kermit and the Muppets*

Sources

Song"; pp. 68-69, "Show Me": Music and Lyrics by Phil Balsam and Dennis Lee

p. 38, "Workin', Workin', Workin'": Music and Lyrics by Don Gillis and Jerry Juhl

pp. 18, 21, "The Minstrels"; p. 58, "The Honk of Honks": Scripts by Jocelyn Stevenson

p. 15, "The Bells of Fraggle Rock": Script by Jocelyn Stevenson (with Jerry Juhl and Susan Juhl)

p. 72, "The Trash Heap Doesn't Live Here Anymore": Script by Jerry Juhl

p. 44, "Movin' Right Along"; pp. 46-47, 73, "The Magic Store": Music and Lyrics by Paul Williams and Kenny Ascher. *The Muppet Movie*.

p. 26; p. 35: Screenplay by Jerry Juhl and Jack Burns. *The Muppet Movie*.

p. 28-29, Screenplay by Frank Oz, Tom Patchett, Jay Tarses. *The Muppets Take Manhattan*.

pp. 62-63, "My Garden": *Kermit's Garden of Verses* by Jack Prelutsky, A Muppet Press Book. Random House Pub. (1982).

Other Material:

pp. 10-11, "Bein' Green": Music and Lyrics by Joe Raposo © 1970 Jonico Music, Inc.; © renewed 1998 by Green Fox Music, Inc. All Rights Reserved. Used by permission.

p. 51, "Frogs in the Glen" by Tony Geiss is administered and licensed by Sesame Workshop. © 1982 Tony Geiss. Used by